Physics

Interactive Reader
Answer Key

Chapter 1 The Science of Physics

REVIEW PREVIOUS CONCEPTS

1. Science is knowledge about the natural world that is based on facts learned through experiments and observation. A scientist is one who makes observations or conducts experiments in pursuit of increasing knowledge.

2. Answers will vary. Students should give examples from their daily lives, both at school and at home.

SECTION 1 WHAT IS PHYSICS?

1. To satisfy their curiosity about the world and to seek new technologies

2. You throw the ball harder, and/or at a steeper angle.

3. An example would be the model of the atom as similar to a sun (nucleus) with planets (electrons).

4. An example would be an illustration of the water cycle.

5. The size of the objects and the height from which they fell

Review

1. a test of a hypothesis that tests only one factor at a time and holds others steady

2. mechanics, thermodynamics, vibrations and wave phenomena, optics, electromagnetism, relativity, and quantum mechanics

3. observing and collecting data, formulating and testing hypotheses, interpreting results and revising the hypothesis, stating conclusions

4. Answers could include diagrams, equations, physical models, and computer simulations.

5. mechanics; thermodynamics

SECTION 2 MEASUREMENTS IN EXPERIMENTS

1. Sample response: As more precision became possible in measuring the initial standards, including recognizing small variations, it made sense to switch to a more uniform standard with less possible variation.

2. 873 microseconds

3. $1 \text{ pg} = 10^{-12} \text{ g}$

4. Sample response: 12.3 g

5. 6 significant figures

6. A, because the values are more spread out.

Practice

A. 5×10^{-5} m

B. 1×10^{-6} s

C. 1.5×10^{8} m

Review

1. Accuracy describes how close a measurement is to the correct value. Precision describes how exact the measurement is.

2. meters; seconds

3. 3×10^{-6} ms

4. 0.67

5. Multiple trials allow scientists to verify that a result is repeatable, making them more confident of the result. They help to identify errors, and provide a larger amount of data to analyze.

SECTION 3 THE LANGUAGE OF PHYSICS

1. Your speed is doubled.

Review

1. $\text{kg} \cdot \text{m/s}^2$

2. 10^{-7}

3. direct

4. 8 kg

CHAPTER 1 REVIEW

1a. electromagnetism, vibrations and wave phenomena

1b. thermodynamics, mechanics

2. the details that the fox is brown and the dog is lazy

3. The size of the unit varied depending on who was doing the measuring.

4a. 3

4b. 5

4c. 4

4d. 6

5. 797 g

6. b and c

7a. 10^{-2} or 10^{-3} m

7b. 10^0 m

7c. 10^1 or 10^2 m

7d. 10^1 m

8a. centimeters

8b. grams

8c. meters

8d. kilometers

8e. kilograms

8f. seconds

9. Yes, because the units of both sides of the equation will be in m/s.

10. 0.90 m/s

11a. 3.00×10^8 m/s

11b. 2.9979×10^8 m/s

12. 11 people

Chapter 2 Motion in One Dimension

REVIEW PREVIOUS CONCEPTS

1. Four are reliably known; the last digit is estimated.
2. The meter, second, and kilogram.
3. A table helps you organize data; a graph helps you visualize it. Both are ways to look for patterns in the data.

SECTION 1 DISPLACEMENT AND VELOCITY

1. The landscape near the tracks
2. −7 cm; negative

Conceptual Challenge

1. **Spacecraft** Their displacements are the same, because their starting and ending positions are the same.
2. **Round Trip** The displacements are equal and opposite.
3. **Book on a Table** The displacement is zero, the average velocity is zero, and the average speed is 0.35 m/s.
4. **Round Trip** The velocities are different because the directions are different.

Practice

A. 2.0 km east
B. 3.00 h
C. 0.43 h

Review

1. 24 s
2. No, because a single distance could correspond to a variety of different positions.

3a. B
3b. A
3c. 40 min
3d. Yes, between 40 and 50 min
3e. No

SECTION 2 ACCELERATION

1. Up
2. 20 cm/s

Practice B

A. 2.2 s

Practice C

A. 21 m

Practice D

A. 19.3 m/s; 29 m
B. −7.5 m/s; 19 m

Practice E

A. 2.51 m/s

Review

1. 0.85 s
2. No. Car A could be accelerating slowly, or negatively, from a high initial speed, while Car B accelerates from a lower initial speed.

3a. 0–25 s, 50–125 s, 200–275 s
3b. Constant and 0 at the three intervals in (a); constant and positive from 25–50 s and 500–575 s; constant and negative from 125–200 s, 275–300 s, and 300–500 s
3c. 0–25 s and 200–275 s
3d. 0–25 s, 50–125 s, 200–275 s

4. No, it moves in a positive direction from 25–200 s (when velocity is positive), and in the negative direction from 275–575 s (when velocity is negative).

SECTION 3 FALLING OBJECTS

1. After 4.0 s
2. 0 at about 1.1 s; decreasing from 0 to 1.1 s; increasing from 1.1 s to 3.00 s

Practice F

A. −42 m/s
B. 11 s

Review

1a. It decreases to zero, then becomes negative and increases in the negative direction.
1b. remain constant
2. She will land at the same speed. Because motion upward and downward will be mirrored, if she has a certain upward velocity at a given height, and then the same downward velocity at that height, her speed at $h = 0$ will be the same.

3a. 0.3 s
3b. 1.4 s
3c. 0.3 s
3d. 0 to 0.3 s
3e. 0.3 to 1.4 s

CHAPTER 2 REVIEW

1a. 5.0 m

1b. +5.0 m

1c. The slope of a line tangent to the graph at that point in time.

2. The displacement of the duck must also be zero. It is back where it started, whether it moved elsewhere during that interval or not.

3a. Acceleration is positive, then negative.

3b. cceleration is zero.

3c. Acceleration is positive.

4. 4.0 s

5. −39.6 m/s

6a. The ball's initial velocity is positive and upward. It slows until it reaches its maximum altitude, then becomes increasingly negative as it falls to the ground.

6b. 0

6c. 9.81 m/s^2

6d. 9.81 m/s^2

7. 2.2×10^2 m

8. −1.5 m/s

9. Yes. If it is slowing down, then its acceleration is opposite to its velocity.

10a. slope is zero

10b. slope is negative

Chapter 3 Two-Dimensional Motion and Vectors

REVIEW PREVIOUS CONCEPTS

1. Displacement is the difference between an object's initial and final positions. It has both magnitude and direction.
2. Velocity is the rate of change of displacement over time.
3. Acceleration is the rate of change of velocity over time.

SECTION 1 INTRODUCTION TO VECTORS

1. Sample scalar: distance; sample vector: displacement
2. $-2\mathbf{v} = -6$ cm/s

Review

1a. vector
1b. scalar
1c. scalar
1d. vector
1e. scalar
2. 126 m at $10°$ above the horizontal
3. 0 m

SECTION 2 VECTOR OPERATIONS

1. $v_y = (\sin \theta)\, v_{plane}$
2. Image should be a right triangle, the horizontal and vertical vectors set head-to-tail, and the hypotenuse running from the open tail to the open head.
3. The displacement would be the same.

Practice A

A. 45.6 m at $9.5°$ east of north

Practice B

A. 12 km/h vertical and 54 km/h horizontal
B. 95 km/h

Practice C

A. 49 m at an angle $7.3°$ to the right of downfield

Review

1. The x-axis horizontal at water level, the y-axis up and down
2. 7.07 km north; 7.07 km east
3. Because the Pythagorean theorem and tangent functions apply only to right triangles

SECTION 3 PROJECTILE MOTION

1. Sketch should be a symmetric upside-down (vertex at top) parabola.
2. Sketch should be several parabolic arcs all starting from the same point.
3. The acceleration due to gravity and any initial vertical component of velocity

Practice D

A. 0.66 m/s
B. 4.9 m/s

Review

1a. yes
1b. yes
1c. no
1d. yes
1e. no
2a. 5.05 s
2b. 454 m
3. 192 m

SECTION 4 PROJECTILE MOTION

1. -170 km/h
2. Sketch should be several parabolic arcs all starting from the same point.
3. The acceleration due to gravity and any initial vertical component of velocity

Conceptual Challenge

1. **Elevator Acceleration** Greater than, because the elevator is accelerating upward toward the ball.
2. **Aircraft Carrier** The plane's relative velocity is slower when it approaches from the stern.

Practice F

A. 14.5 m/s forward

Review

1. There is no change in velocity if you move to an identical walkway. If you move to the floor, there is a sharp change in velocity from 3 m/s to 0 m/s.
2. south with a speed equal to the train's speed
3. appears to fall straight down

CHAPTER 3 REVIEW

1. No, because the scalar has no direction.

2. They are equal and opposite.

3. Yes.

4. To the passenger, the ball appears to move in a straight line. To an observer outside the train, the ball appears to follow a parabola.

5. Yes, the distance from the tail of the first vector to the head of the last vector is zero.

6. 5 blocks at 53° north of east; 13 blocks

7. 2.77×10^5 m

8. the coordinate system in which the motion is described

9a. 70 m/s east

9b. 20 m/s

10. 11 m

11. 1.31 km north; 2.81 km east

12. They form a closed triangle when laid head to tail.

Chapter 4 Forces and the Laws of Motion

SECTION 1 CHANGES IN MOTION

1. **Reading Check** Force can cause a stationary object to move, a moving object to stop, and a moving object to change direction.

2. **Identify** Contact forces: the figure supporting the pieces of paper, a person supporting the balloon; field forces: gravitational force pulling down on the paper and balloon, electric force pulling up on the paper

Practice

Diagrams should include a downward gravitational force and an upward force of the desk on the book; both vectors should have the same length and should be labeled.

Review

1. Sample answers: a. kicking a stationary ball, b. catching a ball, c. hitting a pitched ball with a bat

2. Sample answers: Gravity is an example of a field force, and pulling on a car door to open it is an example of a contact force I use every day.

3. the newton; $1 \text{ N} = 1 \text{ kg} \cdot 1 \text{ m/s}^2$

4. because force has both magnitude and direction

SECTION 2 NEWTON'S FIRST LAW

1. **Reading Check** It remains at rest.

2. **Infer** A bumpy road would have more resistance than a smooth road, so the force due to resistance would increase.

3. **Reading Check** The net force acting on the object must be equal to zero.

Practice

2.48 N at 25.0° counterclockwise from straight down

Review

1. zero

2. −3674 N uphill

3. 4502 N at 1.655° forward of the side

4. No; either no force or two or more forces are required for equilibrium.

SECTION 3 NEWTON'S SECOND AND THIRD LAWS

1. **Reading Check** the net force acting on the object, and the mass of the object.

2. **Reading Check** the forces that two interacting objects exert on each other

Practice

A. 2.2 m/s^2 forward

B. 1.4 m/s^2 north

Review

1a. 12 N

1b. 3.0 m/s^2

2a. person pushes on ground; ground pushes on person

2b. snowball exerts force on back; back exerts force on snowball

2c. ball exerts force on glove; glove exerts force on ball

3. 1.6 m/s^2 at an angle of 65° north of east

SECTION 4 EVERYDAY FORCES

1. **Reading Check** Weight depends on location because it affected by the force due to gravity.

2. **Evaluate** No, both forces act on the television and therefore cannot be an action-reaction pair.

3. **Reading Check** Static friction keeps an object from starting to move; kinetic friction opposes the movement of two surfaces that are in contact.

Practice

A. 0.67

B. 0.52

Review

1. 3.70 N

2. a. 34 N; b. 39 N

3. 0.37, 0.32

CHAPTER 4 REVIEW

1. yes; The object could move at a constant velocity.

2. $F_{applied}$ (185 N) points forward, F_g (155 N) points downward, F_n (155 N) points upward. The diagram may also include $F_{friction}$ backward.

3a. F_g points down, and F_R points up.

3b. F_{rotors} points up, and F_g points down.

3c. F_g points down, F_{track} points in the direction of motion, and F_n points up

4. on the horse: the force of the cart, F_g down, F_n up, a reaction force of the ground on the hooves; on the cart: the force of the horse, F_g down, F_n up, kinetic friction

5. a. zero; b. zero

6. 3.52 m/s^2

7. 55 N to the right

8. Mass is the inertial property of matter. Weight is the gravitational force acting on an object. Weight is equal to mass times the free-fall acceleration.

9. $F_{s,max}$

10a. the weight of the ball and an equal reaction force of the ball on Earth; the force of the person's hand on the ball and an equal reaction force of the ball on the hand; b. *Fg*; the force of the ball on Earth

11. 0.70, 0.60

12. 0.436

13. a. 9.81 m/s^2 downward; b. 22.2 N

14. 64 N upward

15. a. zero; b. 33.9 N

16. −1.2 m/s^2; 0.12

Chapter 5 Forces and the Laws of Motion

REVIEW PREVIOUS CONCEPTS

1. Sample response: $d = vt, d = 0.5at^2, v = at$
2. $F = ma$
3. The friction that acts between a sliding object and a surface, and resists the object's motion

SECTION 1 WORK

1. Sample response: lifting the baseball off the ground, hitting the baseball with a bat
2. $-2v = -6$ cm/s

Practice A

A. 7.0×10^2 J
B. 1.1 m

Review

1a. negative
1b. positive
1c. negative
2. 8.28×10^3 J
3a. yes
3b. no
3c. yes

SECTION 2 ENERGY

1. Increase its speed.
2. negative; decrease
3. It decreases.
4. The second.

Practice B

A. 1.7×10^2 m/s
B. 38.8 m/s

Practice C

A. 7.8 m
B. 3.0×10^2 N

Practice D

A. 3.3 J
B. 3.1×10^2 J
C. 7.5×10^2 J

Review

1. 4.4×10^3 J
2. 0.003 J
3a. kinetic
3b. kinetic and gravitational potential
3c. kinetic and elastic potential

SECTION 3 CONSERVATION OF ENERGY

1. to keep the same
2. decreasing; decreasing; increasing; constant

Practice E

A. 7550 J; 9.9 m/s
B. 0.18 m

Review

1. 0.256 J
2. No, the car cannot go higher than its starting position because this would mean that it somehow gained more energy.
3a. yes
3b. no
3c. yes
4. gravitational potential to kinetic; kinetic energy of the ball to kinetic energy of the wheel

SECTION 4 POWER

1. It increases.

Conceptual Challenge

1. **Mountain Roads** The same amount of energy is needed to reach the top in both cases. Because the same amount of work must be done, the longer path requires more time and therefore less power.
2. **Light Bulbs** Light bulbs don't have energy stored within them. Instead, energy is transferred to them using electricity.

Practice F

A. 2.61×10^8 s, or 8.27 s

Review

1. 12.3 s; 2.45×10^3 J
2. Power equals energy transferred divided by the time to transfer.
3. A powerful engine is capable of doing more work in a given time. The force and speed delivered by a powerful engine are greater than the force and speed of a less powerful engine.

CHAPTER 5 REVIEW

1. The car that took longer to break was moving faster.
2. Work must be done against gravity to climb a staircase at a constant speed. Walking on a horizontal surface does not require work to be done against gravity.
3. 53 J
4. 7.6×10^4 J
5a. yes, positive
5b. no
5c. yes, positive
5d. yes, negative
6a. nonmechanical
6b. mechanical
6c. mechanical
6d. mechanical
6e. both
7. 3600 J; 12.0 m/s
8. The ball will not hit the lecturer because according to the conservation of mechanical energy, it cannot end with a greater energy than it started with. If the lecturer pushes the ball, this adds more energy and the ball can rise higher than if it were dropped.
9. 5.9×10^8 W
10. 17.2 s
11. at the ball's lowest height; at the ball's maximum height

Chapter 6 Momentum and Collisions

REVIEW PREVIOUS CONCEPTS

1. The object will accelerate in the direction of the net force.
2. The object's mass and speed are used to determine the energy of motion.
3. Energy can change form but can never be created or destroyed.

SECTION 1 MOMENTUM AND IMPULSE

1. The momentum will also be due east.
2. Even if it is moving slowly, the large mass of the barge will mean a large momentum if it runs into the dock.
3. The bird would have more momentum. The elephant standing still would have zero momentum because it is not moving.
4. The team with the shift in momentum seems to have things moving in their direction.
5. At a higher speed, the same force would require more distance to bring the car to a stop.

Practice

A. 6.66 m/s to the south
Ba. 1.2×10^2 kg·m/s to the northwest
Bb. 94 kg·m/s to the northwest
Bc. 27 kg·m/s to the northwest
C. 38 N to the left
D. 16 kg·m/s to the south
E. 4.05 s
F. 32 N to the left

Review

1a. momentum increases by a factor of 2
1b. kinetic energy increases by a factor of 4
2a. 4.5 kg·m/s
2b. 31 m/s
3. 2.6 kg·m/s downfield
4. No, because it is possible for a large force applied over a very short interval to change the momentum less than a smaller force applied over a longer period of time.

SECTION 2 CONSERVATION OF MOMENTUM

1. The momentum gain by Earth is down, opposite to the gain in momentum as you jump up.
2. The negative sign indicates that the reaction force is opposite in direction to the action force.
3. The negative sign indicates that the change in momentum of the first object is in the opposite direction to the change in momentum of the second object.

Practice

A. 1.90 m/s toward the spacecraft
B. 38 kg

Review

1a. The ball will move away from the student at 7.0 m/s horizontally.
1b. The student and the ball will move to the right at 1.5 m/s.
2. 61 m/s.
3a. Yes. The momentum lost by one object must be equal to the momentum gained by the other object.
3b. No. The final velocity of the second object also depends on the initial velocity of the second object and the mass of the first object.
3c. Yes. Using the conservation of momentum, you could substitute the given values and solve for the final velocity of the other object.

SECTION 3 ELASTIC AND INELASTIC COLLISIONS

1. The negative sign indicates that the object is moving to the west.
2. No. The total kinetic energy will decrease if no external forces are added to the system.
3. In an elastic collision, the total kinetic energy is conserved. In a perfectly inelastic collision, the total kinetic energy always decreases.

Practice

A. 3.8 m/s to the south

B. 4.2 m/s to the right

Ca. 0.43 m/s to the west

Cb. 17 J

Da. 6.2 m/s to the south

Db. 3.9 J

Review

1. For elastic collisions, answers may include billiard balls colliding, a soccer ball hitting a player's foot, or a tennis ball hitting a wall. For perfectly inelastic collisions, answers may include a person catching a ball, a meteorite hitting Earth, or two clay balls colliding.

2a. 1.1 m/s to the south

2b. 1.4×10^3 J

3. No. Some of the KE is converted to sound energy, and some is converted to internal elastic potential energy as the cars deform, so the collision is not elastic.

CHAPTER 6 REVIEW

1. zero

2. No. Objects with the same kinetic energy must also have the same mass and the same direction to have the same momentum.

3. A floor mat decreases the average force on the gymnast by increasing the time interval in which the gymnast is brought to rest.

4a. The net velocity of all insects must be zero, although each insect could be moving.

4b. The velocity of each insect must be zero.

5. 7.50×10^2 kg· m/s to the southwest

6. 18 N, 4.4 kg· m/s

7. 0.010 s

8. Before they push, the total momentum of the system is zero. So, after they push, the total momentum of the system must remain zero.

9. 1 m/s

10. 4.0 m/s

11. 42.0 m/s toward second base

12. 14.5 m/s to the north

13. 0.83 m/s to the right

Chapter 7 Circular Motion and Gravitation

REVIEW PREVIOUS CONCEPTS

1. the rate of change of displacement; the rate of change of velocity
2. a net force on the object
3. The mechanical energy can change.

SECTION 1 CIRCULAR MOTION

1. 16π m, twice your speed
2. tangential acceleration
3. to the right

Practice

A. 2.5 m/s
B. 3.08 m/s^2
C. 40.0 N

Review

1. Answers will vary.
2. Answers will vary, but should indicate that centripetal acceleration changes direction and tangential acceleration changes speed.
3. inertia

SECTION 2 NEWTON'S LAW OF UNIVERSAL GRAVITATION

1. Earth is much more massive than the book.
2. It decreases.
3. the mass of a planet or other massive object and distance from its center

Practice

A. 0.692 m
B. 38.5 N

Conceptual Challenge

1. **Gravity on the Moon** No, because the distance from the center of the moon to its surface is less than the distance from the center of Earth to its surface, and distance also determines g.
2. **Selling Gold** Weight decreases as altitude increases, so the scam artist should buy at high altitude and sell at low altitude.

Review

1. Gravity provides the centripetal acceleration to keep the satellite from moving off in a line tangent to its orbit.
2. 6.5 m/s^2
3. 5.98×10^{24} kg

SECTION 3 MOTION IN SPACE

1. We now believe that objects orbit the sun, not Earth, and in ellipses, not circles.
2. It increases.
3. 400 N

Practice

A. 1.90×10^6 m

Review

1. Newton's theory of universal gravitation provided a mechanism to explain Kepler's descriptions of planetary motion.
2. Because the moon has a smaller mass and smaller radius than Earth
3. Apparent weightlessness; they are in free-fall.

SECTION 4 TORQUE AND SIMPLE MACHINES

1. the middle of her body, where her center of mass is
2. a day; a year

Practice

A. 0.75 N·m
B. 133 N

Review

1. Answers will vary.
2. It would increase.
3. Answers will vary. Possibilities might include the wheel and axle for the wheels or the gears, levers for the brakes, pulleys for the gears.

CHAPTER 7 REVIEW

1. No; there must be centripetal acceleration to keep it on a curved path.

2. The satellite is also moving parallel to Earth's surface, at such a speed that Earth's surface curves away from it at the same rate the satellite falls.

3. Neither one; they have the same orbital speed.

4. Placing the axis of rotation nearer to the rock will increase the mechanical advantage.

5. 7.0 m/s

6. 2.50 m

7. F_2

8. 26 N·m

9. 1630 m/s

10. No, because the forces act at the same point, so the net force is 0.

11. The longer screwdriver provides a longer lever arm and greater mechanical advantage.

12. 0, because the normal force it exerts to hold you up is zero.

Chapter 8 Fluid Mechanics

REVIEW PREVIOUS CONCEPTS

1. shape and velocity
2. Mechanical energy is constant.
3. Total mass is constant.

SECTION 1 FLUIDS AND BUOYANT FORCE

1. liquids and gases
2. Divide the mass by the volume.
3. The weight is downward, and the buoyant force is upward. The weight is greater than the buoyant force.
4. 0 N
5. Object floats: $\rho_f > \rho_o$; Object sinks: $\rho_f < \rho_o$; Object is suspended: $\rho_f = \rho_o$

Practice

A. 3.57×10^3 kg/m^3
B. 6.4×10^2 kg/m^3

Review

1. A solid has a definite shape, while a fluid does not. A liquid has a definite volume, while a gas does not.

2a. no

2b. yes

2c. yes

2d. yes

3. The kayak's effective density includes the material of the kayak itself and the air within the kayak. Taken together, these are less than the density of the water.

SECTION 2 FLUID PRESSURE

1. Pressure is force per unit area. Newtons are units of force, and m^2 are units of area.
2. two times larger
3. Gauge pressure is less than total pressure.

Practice

A. 1.48×10^3 N
B. 1.88×10^5 Pa

Review

1. a
2. 5.1×10^6 Pa
3. 20.1 m

SECTION 3 FLUIDS IN MOTION

1. An ideal fluid has no internal friction (non-viscous) and is incompressible.
2. The law of conservation of mass
3. The area of the water stream decreases, so the velocity of the water increases.

Review

1. 16.0 m/s
2. 2.7 m/s
3. 30.0 s, because the volume rate of flow is constant
4. shorter

CHAPTER 8 REVIEW

1. the pascal; 1 pascal (1 Pa) = 1 N/m^2
2. In the ocean; because $\rho_{seawater} > \rho_{fresh\ water}$, less sea water must be displaced.
3. The average density of the boat, including air inside the hollow hull, is less than the density of the water.
4. No; a force on a small area can produce a large pressure.
5. The force opposing F_g is spread out over a large number of nails, so no single nail exerts very much pressure.
6. The moving air above the ball creates a low pressure area so that the air below the ball exerts a force that is equal and opposite F_g.
7. The buoyant force causes the net force on the astronaut to be close to zero. In space, the astronauts accelerate at the same rate as the craft, so they feel as if they have no net force acting on them.

8a. 6.3×10^3 kg/m^3

8b. 9.2×10^2 kg/m^3

9. 14 N downward

10a. 84 g/s

10b. 2.8×10^{-2} cm/s

Chapter 9 Heat

REVIEW PREVIOUS CONCEPTS

1. Work is the product of displacement and the component of the force that is in the same direction as the displacement.
2. Kinetic energy is energy of motion of an object. Potential energy is the energy associated with an object due to its position, shape, or condition.
3. The total mechanical energy of a closed system is conserved in the absence of friction.

SECTION 1 TEMPERATURE AND THERMAL EQUILIBRIUM

1. The temperature usually increases.
2. Only then can the measure of the average kinetic energy of a material be known or represented by the temperature shown on a thermometer.
3. The bottle would crack, because water expands as it freezes. With the bottle sealed, the pressure of the expanding water would likely crack the glass.

Practice
A. −89.22°C, 183.93 K
B. 55K, 99°F

Review
1. The pan's temperature decreases if the water's temperature increases. The water and pan have reached thermal equilibrium when their temperatures are the same.
2a. 119.0°C
2b. melting point = 246.2°F;
    boiling point = 832.3°F
2c. melting point = 392.2 K;
    boiling point = 717.8 K
3. c, a, b; the particles on the left in (c) have the greatest average kinetic energy and therefore have the highest temperature.

SECTION 2 DEFINING HEAT

1. higher, lower
2. Since the particles that make up the two materials still collide and contact each other, transfer of energy still continues.

3. Heat moves by conduction from the flame to the brick or other materials surrounding the fire. Heat moves by convection as currents of warming and cooling air are set up. Heat also moves through the air by radiation.

Practice
A. 1.76×10^3 J
B. 0.96 J

Review
1. In the first case, molecules in the exhaled air have a greater average kinetic energy than the air surrounding you cold hands. Energy is transferred to the cold hands, causing their temperature to increase. In the second case, the molecules in the soup have a greater average kinetic energy than the exhaled air passing over the soup's surface. Energy is therefore transferred from the soup to the relatively cooler air.
2. Yes, shaking the bottle adds kinetic energy to the system, and this kinetic energy is converted to the internal energy of the water molecules.
3. 2.48×10^5 J
4. You would need to know the comparative temperature changes for each bottle of water (assuming that the water does not freeze in either case).

SECTION 3 CHANGES IN TEMPERATURE AND PHASE

1. The high specific heat capacity of water causes it to hold more of its heat for a longer period of time than air. So the water feels warm even after the air has cooled.
2. Water's specific heat capacity is known, so the change in the water's temperature can be used to determine a substance's specific heat capacity.
3. They indicate the times when the substance was undergoing a phase change.

Practice E
A. 47°C
B. 390 J/kg·°C

Review

1. 6.8 g
2. 3340 J
3. When firewood is damp, a large amount of energy is used to increase the water's temperature and then to vaporize the water (because water has both a high specific heat capacity and a high latent heat of vaporization). After this has been accomplished, the remaining energy is used to burn the wood. Thus, much more energy is required when the wood is damp.

CHAPTER 9 REVIEW

1. Temperature increases as the internal energy increases, except during a phase change.
2. Their temperatures are the same.
3. constant temperature points, such as water's melting point and boiling point at 1 atm
4. 56.7°C, 329.8 K
5. when the air temperature is 35°C
6. Air is an insulator, so the internal energy of your body is not as easily transferred to the environment.
7. Heat is energy in transit, not a substance. Temperature is proportional to internal energy, not to heat.
8. The bridge's surface is directly exposed to the cold air both above and below, whereas the road's surface is exposed only on one side. In addition, the stable temperature of the ground below the road helps to keep the road's temperature stable.
9. Evaporation requires energy and thus cools the surrounding air. A fan continuously supplies new, dry air, so perspiration is continually evaporated and the body is cooled.
10. 2.9 J
11. Conservation of energy; energy removed from the sample equals the energy added to the water.
12. Evaporation requires energy, which comes from the air.
13. A large mass of cool earth around the cellar does not undergo as large a temperature change during the year as does the outside air.
14. 25.0°C
15. 14 m

Chapter 10 Thermodynamics

REVIEW PREVIOUS CONCEPTS

1. Work is the product of force and displacement.
2. Internal energy is the sum of the kinetic and potential energies of all the particles in an object or a substance.
3. Heat is the energy transferred from an area of higher temperature to an area of lower temperature until thermal equilibrium is reached.

SECTION 1 RELATIONSHIPS BETWEEN HEAT AND WORK

1. The internal energy increases.
2. The work equation applies only if the pressure is constant.
3. combustion reaction; pressure and temperature increases, volume does not change
4. An isothermal process does not affect the internal energy of an ideal gas.

Practice

A. -4.8×10^5 J
B. 3.3×10^2 J

Review

1. b; energy is transferred as heat to the firecracker, which does work when it explodes.
2. 8.1×10^{-2} J
3a. adiabatic
3b. isothermal
3c. isovolumetric

SECTION 2 THE FIRST LAW OF THERMODYNAMICS

1. *PE* increases and *KE* decreases moving up a hill. *PE* decreases and *KE* increases moving down a hill.
2. isothermal; adiabatic
3. $Q = \Delta U + W; W = Q - \Delta U$
4. Both processes are cyclic. A refrigerator uses mechanical work to transfer energy as heat. A heat engine uses heat to do mechanical work.

Practice

A. 33 J
B. -143 J; removed as heat

Review

1. By definition, no energy is transferred to or from isolated systems, so $Q = W = 0$ and $\Delta U = Q - W = 0$.
2a. $Q = W$
2b. $\Delta U = -W$
2c. $\Delta U = Q$
3a. $W = 3.5 \times 10^2$ J
3b. $\Delta U = -3.6 \times 10^2$ J
3c. adiabatic
4. $Q = -16$ J (removed as heat)

SECTION 3 THE SECOND LAW OF THERMODYNAMICS

1. All heat engines operating in a cycle expel some energy, so $Q_c > 0$.

Practice

A. 0.1504
B. 0.59
C. 5.3×10^3 J

Review

1. no; In order for a heat engine to do work in a thermodynamic cycle, some energy must be transferred as heat to surroundings at a temperature lower than that of the engine.
2. Answers may vary. One example is water freezing in winter (energy transfer from water to air increases air's entropy).
3. Increasing the temperature of the steam increases the amount of energy transferred to the engine as heat (Q_h) and thus raises the engine's efficiency.

CHAPTER 10 REVIEW

1. Energy transfers to the system as heat or as work.

2a. ΔU

2b. Q

2c. W

3. 1.08×10^3 J; done by the gas

4. 3.50×10^2 J

5a. $\Delta U = 0, Q = W$

5b. $\Delta U = -W, Q = 0$

5c. $\Delta U = Q, W = 0$

6. 647 kJ

7. a

8. The plant's efficiency would increase, but the advantage gained would be more than offset by the use of energy needed to refrigerate the water.

9. no; Entropy of water and air during the water's evaporation increases by more than the entropy of the sodium and chloride ions decreases.

10. 0.210

11. 0.32

Chapter 11 Vibrations and Waves

REVIEW PREVIOUS CONCEPTS

1. the energy stored in a stretched or compressed elastic object
2. The spring is stiff and resists being stretched or compressed.
3. the energy associated with an object due to the object's position relative to a gravitational source

SECTION 1 SIMPLE HARMONIC MOTION

1. at maximum displacement
2. At maximum displacement, the spring force and acceleration are at a maximum, and the speed of the mass is zero.
3. to the right
4. The elastic potential energy of the bow is greater than the kinetic energy of the arrow because some of the potential energy was converted to kinetic energy of the bow and bowstring.
5. It must be proportional to the displacement.
6. In both systems, the restoring force is zero at the equilibrium position.
7. at maximum displacement

Practice

A. 570 N/m
B. stiffer

Review

1. c
2. 0.52 N
3. because the acrobat's momentum carries him or her through the equilibrium position

SECTION 2 MEASURING SIMPLE HARMONIC MOTION

1. 0.1 Hz
2. the length of the pendulum and the free-fall acceleration
3. the mass and the spring constant
4. no, because the period is proportional to the square root of the mass

Practice

A. 1.4×10^2 m
B. 0.25 m
C. 1.0×10^{-2} kg
D. 1.7 s, 0.59 Hz

Review

1. 3.0 Hz, 0.33 s
2a. 3.2 s
2b. 0.31 Hz
3a. 25 N/m
3b. 1.1 s

SECTION 3 PROPERTIES OF WAVES

1. waves that require a material medium
2. a special case of a periodic wave in which the periodic motion is simple harmonic
3. The wave moves to the right, but the marked point moves up and down.
4. The particles of the medium move perpendicularly to the wave motion.
5. The crest is the highest point above the equilibrium position, and the trough is the lowest point below the equilibrium position.
6. The particles of the medium move parallel to the wave motion.
7. The frequency is halved.

Practice

A. 346 m/s
B. 5.86 m

Review

1. The disturbance moves, not the medium.
2. 6.0×10^4 Hz

SECTION 4 WAVE INTERACTIONS

1. 6 cm

2. when there is a superposition of waves in which the displacements are on the same side of the equilibrium position

3. The pulses that result in destructive interference have displacements that are on opposite sides of the equilibrium position, not on the same side.

4. Particles in a compression are closer together, and particles in a rarefaction are farther apart.

5. at the nodes

Review

1. 0.50 m

2. Wavelengths that will produce standing waves include 4.0 m, 2.0 m, and 1.3 m; Any value that does not allow both ends of the string to be nodes is acceptable.

CHAPTER 11 REVIEW

1. oscillation about an equilibrium position in which a restoring force is proportional to displacement

2. No, acceleration changes throughout the oscillator's motion. It is zero at the equilibrium position and greatest at maximum displacement.

3. because frictional forces are neglected in an ideal mass-spring system

4. 4A

5. They are inversely related.

6. Transverse wave particles vibrate perpendicular to wave motion. Longitudinal wave particles vibrate parallel to wave motion.

7. 1/3 s; 3 Hz

8. In constructive interference, individual displacements are on the same side of the equilibrium position. In destructive interference, the individual displacements are on opposite sides of the equilibrium position.

9. 1.75 m, 3.5 m, and 7.0 m

10. becomes $\sqrt{2}$ times as long; remains the same because mass does not affect period

11a. 0.57 s

11b. 1.8 Hz

12a. 9.0 cm

12b. 20.0 cm

12c. 0.0400 s

12d. 5.00 m/s

Chapter 12 Sound

REVIEW PREVIOUS CONCEPTS

1. parallel
2. λ stands for wavelength; f stands for frequency

SECTION 1 SOUND WAVES

1. Particles in the medium vibrate parallel to the direction of the wave motion.
2. A dog whistle produces sounds at frequencies outside the range that humans can hear.
3. Frequency is an objective count of how fast particles vibrate in a certain amount of time. Pitch is subjective and depends on how the listener hears the sound.
4. 100°C
5. Observer B

Review

1. Answers may vary. A compression is an area of relatively high pressure or particle density. A rarefaction is an area of relatively low pressure or particle density.
2. A greater frequency is perceived as a higher pitch.
3. Sound waves travel faster through water than through air because the molecules of water are closer together and, as a result, can spread vibrations more quickly.
4. to the right
5. The dolphin is catching up to the fish.

SECTION 2 SOUND INTENSITY AND RESONANCE

1. The sound intensity energy gets less and less as the energy is distributed over a larger and larger area.
2. no; Those sounds are too low in frequency for an average person to hear.
3. a buzzing mosquito
4. the last (rightmost) one

Practice

A. 6.4×10^{-3} W/m^2
B. 8.91×10^{-3} W/m^2
C. 4.8 m

Review

1. Answers may vary. Intensity is the rate at which energy flows through a given area.
2. Intensity has increased by a factor of 100 (10^2).
3. no; because the sensation of loudness is approximately logarithmic in the human ear
4. Students should circle a, d, and f. They should draw boxes around c and e.

SECTION 3 HARMONICS

1. The fundamental frequency of a vibrating string is the lowest frequency of a standing wave for that string.
2. Harmonics are integral multiples of the fundamental frequency.
3. They make the vibrating strings or air columns longer or shorter.
4. Open pipes have all harmonics. Pipes that are closed at one end have only odd numbered harmonics.
5. Each instrument has different harmonics at different intensities.
6. Two sound waves are out of phase when the compressions overlap with the rarefactions of the other, causing destructive interference.

Practice

A. 440 Hz
B. 260 Hz, 520 Hz, 780 Hz

Review

1. A harmonic series is a series of frequencies that includes the fundamental frequency and its integral multiples.
2. 524 Hz
3. 348 m/s
4. the odd harmonics
5. a, b

CHAPTER 12 REVIEW

1. Molecules that have more motion (higher temperature) can transfer their vibrations more easily. This is less noticeable in liquids and solids because the particles are closer together.

2. The siren's pitch will drop.

3. Sound travels faster through the ground than through the air.

4. Intensity is power per area; decibel level is a measure of *relative* intensity.

5. 90 dB, 30 dB, 60 dB (Answers may vary slightly.)

6. when a forced vibration is the same as the natural frequency of a vibrating system

7. 9 machines (for a total of 10)

8. because a closed end is a node, while an open end is an antinode

9. The instruments have different harmonics present at various intensity levels.

10. The guitar's body transfers the string's vibrations to the air more efficiently, which increases the intensity of the sound.

11. As temperature increases, the speed of sound in air increases. Because f_1 is proportional to v, fundamental frequency likewise increases.

12. 443 Hz, 886 Hz, 1330 Hz

13. 5 beats per second

14. 70.1 Hz

Chapter 13 Light and Reflection

REVIEW PREVIOUS CONCEPTS

1. wavelength, frequency, speed;
   speed = wavelength × frequency
   (or any variation of this equation)
2. energy

SECTION 1 CHARACTERISTICS OF LIGHT

1. Visible light is electromagnetic radiation. It is only a very small part of the electromagnetic spectrum.
2. Light from the sun spreads out as the square of the distance from the sun. Mars is more distant from the sun than Earth. Thus sunlight is more spread out and the illumination on Mars is less than on Earth.

Practice

A. 3.4 m
B. 5.4×10^{14} Hz

Review

1. As frequency increases, wavelength becomes less. The speed remains the same.
2. 7.41×10^{14} Hz
3. An electromagnetic wave consists of oscillating electric and magnetic fields perpendicular to each other and to the direction of wave travel.

SECTION 2 FLAT MIRRORS

1. Light can be either absorbed or reflected.
2. The room will appear twice as large. Every object in the room will have a corresponding virtual image the same size behind the mirror.

Review

1. The image is behind the mirror, the same distance as the object is in front of the mirror. It is the same size as the object.
2. In diffuse reflection, the reflected light rays are scattered in many directions. In specular reflection, rays are reflected in one direction.
3. ray, perpendicular, reflection, incidence, reflection (Last two responses can be in either order.)

SECTION 3 CURVED MIRRORS

1. The light rays must come together at a point.
2. Light rays that strike a convex mirror always diverge. Such a mirror cannot cause light rays to converge to form a real image.

Practice

A. $q = 53$ cm; $M = -0.57$; real, inverted image
B. $R = 1.00 \times 10^2$ cm; $M = 2.00$; virtual image

Review

1a. concave spherical
1b. flat and convex spherical
1c. concave spherical
2. Concave spherical mirrors suffer from spherical aberration. They cannot focus a star image at a single point.
3. $q = 42.9$ cm, $M = 0.715$

SECTION 4 COLOR AND POLARIZATION

1. The electric fields of unpolarized light oscillate in random directions. The fields of polarized light oscillate in only one direction.

Review

1. yellow
2. magenta
3. scattering by air molecules
4. horizontal

CHAPTER 13 REVIEW

1. Ultraviolet light has the highest frequency. Radio waves have the longest wavelength.
2. The apparent brightness is less. Apparent brightness equals the actual brightness divided by the square of the distance between observer and source.
3. The wavelength of blue light is smaller. The frequency of blue light is higher. Their speeds are equal.
4. 9.1×10^{-3} m (9.1 mm)
5. a. diffuse; b. specular; c. specular; d. diffuse
6. Your image is behind the mirror at a distance of 2 m. The magnification is 1, because the image is the same size as the object.

7a. real

7b. farther away than the object, beyond the center of curvature

7c. taller than the object

7d. inverted

8. The pigments are cyan, magenta, and yellow. When mixed, they produce black.

9. a. red;

   b. black

10. Look at the clear sky through the glasses while rotating them. If the sky becomes darker, the glasses are polarized.

11. The mirror is convex. Objects you see are virtual images that are reduced in size. Your brain interprets the smaller images as being farther away.

12. Place a white card or sheet of paper where the image appears. If the image is projected on the sheet, it is a real image.

13. A concave spherical mirror can form either a virtual image or a real image depending on the position of the object. If the object is near the mirror, a virtual image appears behind the mirror. If the object is farther away, a real image forms in front of the mirror.

14. A spherical mirror exhibits spherical aberration in which rays striking the mirror near the edges do not focus at the image position. A parabolic mirror eliminates this problem.

15. Light can be polarized by scattering in the atmosphere and by reflecting from a shiny surface.

Chapter 14 Refraction

REVIEW PREVIOUS CONCEPTS

1. speed = wavelength × frequency, or variations of this equation
2. The focal point is the point at which parallel rays (as from the sun) come to a focus. The focal length is the distance from the mirror to the focal point.

SECTION 1 REFRACTION

1. Refraction is the bending of light as it passes from one material into another at an angle. Refraction occurs because the speed of light in one material is different from the speed in another material.
2. Diamonds and cubic zirconia crystals have almost equal indices of refraction. Therefore, they look similar in the way they refract light.
3. You would reach deeper than where the image appears to be.

Practice

A. 18.5°
B. 12.5°

Review

1. a, d
2. 6.14°
3a. away
3b. toward
3c. toward
3d. away

SECTION 2 THIN LENSES

1. A converging lens is convex. A diverging lens is concave.
2. A converging lens forms a virtual image when the object is nearer than the focal length of the lens.

Practice

A. 20.0 cm behind lens, $M = -1.00$; real, inverted image, same size as the object.
B. −30.0 cm (behind the lens), $M = 3.00$; virtual, upright image, larger than the object

Review

1. real, inverted
2. 9.3 cm
3a. virtual, upright
3b. real, inverted

SECTION 3 OPTICAL PHENOMENA

1. On hot days, there are differences in the density, thus the refractive index, of air. These differences cause the atmospheric refraction needed to form mirages.

Review

1. b, d, e
2. Green light will be bent more. The amount of refraction depends on wavelength. Shorter wavelengths refract more.
3. It is evening. The sun must be behind the man (in the west).

CHAPTER 14 REVIEW

1. A light ray bends toward the normal when the speed of light in the second medium is lower than in the first medium. (The second medium has a higher index of refraction than the first.)
2a. The frequency does not change.
2b. The wavelength becomes shorter.
2c. The speed decreases.
3. The index of refraction increases when the speed of light slows down in a medium.
   or:
   $$\text{index of refraction} = \frac{\text{speed of light in vacuum}}{\text{speed of light in medium}}$$
4. No, refraction occurs only when the light ray is at an angle with the normal.
5. 26°
6. You would use a converging lens and place the lens over the flammable object at a distance equal to the focal length of the lens. This is the position at which parallel rays from a distant object will focus to a point.
7a. The object is farther away than the focal point.
7b. The object is closer than the focal point.
7c. The object is farther away than the focal point.
7d. The object is closer than the focal point.

8. The focal length will be longer because light rays passing from the water into the glass lens will not refract as much as they would when passing from air into the lens. Therefore, the rays come to a focus farther from the lens.

9. The objective lens forms a real, inverted image of the object. The eyepiece simply acts as a magnifier of that real image.

10a. chromatic aberration

10b. spherical aberration

11. Mirages usually occur during hot, sunny conditions.

12. Light rays entering the diamond are dispersed into visible colors because of the high index of refraction of diamond.

13. You would install a diverging lens in order to see a virtual image of a wide area outside the door.

14. Blue light is refracted the most. The shorter the wavelength, the greater the refraction. Of the colors mentioned, blue light has the shortest wavelength.

Chapter 15 Interference and Diffraction

REVIEW PREVIOUS CONCEPTS

1. The waves combine and interfere either constructively or destructively.
2. The waves interfere constructively (reinforce) when they meet in phase. The waves interfere destructively (cancel) when they meet out of phase.

SECTION 1 INTERFERENCE

1. In part (a), the waves are in phase, so they add to each other, producing a wave of greater amplitude. In part (b), the waves are out of phase and partially cancel each other, producing a wave of reduced amplitude.

2a. constructive interference, producing a wave of higher amplitude

2b. destructive interference, resulting in a wave of reduced amplitude or complete cancellation if the interfering waves are of equal amplitude

3. one, one

4. The two waves arrive at the screen out of phase.

5. The second-order maxima lie farther outward from the central maximum than the first-order maxima.

Practice

A. 574 nm

B. 5.1×10^{-7} m $= 5.1 \times 10^2$ nm

Review

1a. For constructive interference, the path length must differ by a whole number multiple of one wavelength.

1b. For destructive interference, the path length must differ by an odd number multiple of half wavelengths..

2. Only monochromatic (single wavelength) light will interfere in specific positions on the screen to give a sharp pattern. The different colors of non-monochromatic ligt will interfere at different positions, giving a blurred pattern.

3. 0.125°

SECTION 2 DIFFRACTION

1. Sound of a lower pitch has a longer wavelength. The longer the wavelength of the sound waves, the better they can bend (diffract) around large objects such as rocks, small islands, and other ships.

2. Every portion of the slit can act as a source of waves. Light from the different portions can interfere as if it were from two closely spaced sources.

3. The wavelength of the light determines the position of the line.

4. The shorter the wavelength of light, the smaller the angle of resolution, and the greater the resolving power.

Practice

A. 0.02°, 0.04°

B. 17.2°

C. 6.62×10^3 lines/cm

Review

1a. $5.89 \times 10{-7}$ m (589 nm)

1b. 24.7°

2. a human hair because it is closer in size to the wavelength of visible light

3. yes; Ultraviolet light has a shorter wavelength than visible light, and resolving power is greater for shorter wavelengths.

4. If the hole is big enough, you would see a sharp shadow of the edges of the hole. As the hole is made smaller, diffraction would begin around the edges, giving a larger, fuzzier light spot. When the hole is very small you would see a wide diffraction pattern.

SECTION 3 LASERS

1. It cannot be coherent because it consists of many different wavelengths that have many different phase relationships.

2. All the light waves emitted by the laser travel in the same direction.

Review

1. Both are monochromatic but the waves of laser light are in phase and remain in phase over time.

2. Laser light is monochromatic, coherent, and forms a single narrow beam that does not spread out. Light from an incandescent bulb has none of these properties.

3a. wavelength

3b. monochromatic

3c. coherent

3d. in phase

3e. constructive

3f. energy state

3g. stimulated emission

CHAPTER 15 REVIEW

1. When the waves interfere constructively, the resultant wave has twice the amplitude (brightness). When they interfere destructively, the waves cancel leaving no resultant wave (darkness).

2. by differences in brightness

3. Interference fringes form at smaller angles for blue light because it has shorter wavelength than red light.

4. 630 nm

5. no, because their light is neither monochromatic nor coherent

6. Different parts of the slit act as new light sources. Light from these parts of the slit interfere with each other, forming dark fringes where they interfere destructively and light fringes where they interfere constructively.

7. Light with longer wavelength is diffracted more, so the width of the central region increases.

8. Each different color (wavelength) is diffracted at a different angle, so the colors are separated on the screen.

9. The separation becomes greater as the number of lines per centimeter increases. So the second grating that produces the wider pattern has greater number of lines.

10. 3.22°

11. 3.22°

12. Laser light is coherent and monochromatic. It also travels in a narrow beam in one direction.

13. Light must be coherent for an interference pattern to form. An interference pattern is well defined (sharp) with monochromatic light.

Chapter 16 Electric Forces and Fields

REVIEW PREVIOUS CONCEPTS

1. Vectors can be added graphically, or by finding the x- and y-components of each vector and adding them to find the x- and y-components of the resultant.
2. It can act on an object at a distance, with no need for contact.
3. in the nucleus; in orbit around the nucleus

SECTION 1 ELECTRIC CHARGE

1. Because plastic is good at attracting extra electrons, the plastic slide is negatively charged and the child is positively charged.
2. repel

Review

1. positive; equal to the magnitude of the negative charge on the rod
2. Electric charge is quantized.
3. The surface of the tape becomes charged as it is pulled away. The charged tape then polarizes nearby sections of the desk.

SECTION 2 ELECTRIC FORCE

1. It is quadrupled.
2. They must be equal.

Practice

A. 2.2×10^{-5} N, attractive
B. 3.0×10^{-6} N, to the left
C. 24.5 cm from q_1 (15.5 cm from q_2)

Review

1. 4.4 N, attractive
2. The distance between them decreased, by a factor of 3.
3. Both are field forces and follow inverse square laws. Electric force is stronger than the gravitational force, and can be attractive or repulsive rather than just attractive.

SECTION 3 THE ELECTRIC FIELD

1. the mass of Earth
2a. up and left
2b. down and right
2c. mostly up
2d. mostly down
2e. up and left
2f. down and right

Practice

A. 3.2×10^{-15} N, along the positive x-axis

Review

1. All field lines should point away from the two charges, and one charge should have four times as many lines as the other.
2a. 3/8
2b. q_2 is positive and q_1 is negative
3. because charge accumulates at sharp points

CHAPTER 16 REVIEW

1. No; the designations 'positive' and 'negative' are arbitrary.
2. Protons are bound in the nucleus; electrons are largely free to move between atoms.
3. The comb has a far greater mass, so its acceleration in response to the force is tiny.
4. 45 N; attractive
5. Because at any point in space, the electric field points in only one direction.
6. The balloon induces a local surface charge on the wall next to it. As a whole, the wall is not charged.
7. to the left
8. 2.2×10^{13} electrons
9. Charge accumulates more densely along the sharper end, leading to a stronger electric field at that point, which interacts with the air around the conductor.
10. Lines should originate on the $+q$ charge and terminate on the $-3q$ charge. There should be three times as many lines connected to the $-3q$ charge.
11. 12.0×10^3 N/C, toward the smaller charge

Chapter 17 Electrical Energy and Current

REVIEW PREVIOUS CONCEPTS

1. Contact forces result from physical contact between two objects. Field forces do not require physical contact between objects.
2. Power is the rate at which energy is transferred or the rate at which work is done.

SECTION 1 ELECTRIC POTENTIAL

1. The charge must move in the same direction as the field.
2. The potential energy would increase if a positive charge moved opposite the direction of **E.**
3. V/m
4. The electric potential decreases as the distance r from the source of the field increases.

Practice

1. $q = 8.0 \times 10^{-19}$ C
2. -54 V
3. -2.8×10^4 V

Review

1. charge, electric field strength, and displacement parallel to the field
2. Mechanical energy is conserved in the absence of friction and radiation.
3. the initial position
4. -6.0×10^{-4} J
5a. -4.0×10^4 V
5b. -6.4×10^{-15} J
6. Electrical potential energy at a point depends on the charge located at that point, while the electric potential at any point is independent of the charge at the point.

SECTION 2 CAPACITANCE

1. The capacitance of a parallel-plate capacitor depends on the area of each plate, the distance between the plates, and the material (if any) between the plates. The capacitance of an isolated conducting sphere depends on the radius of the sphere and the Coulomb constant.

2. The work required to charge a capacitor is equal to the electrical potential energy stored in the capacitor. Three ways to calculate this energy are: $PE_{electric} = \frac{1}{2} Q\Delta V$, $PE_{electric} = \frac{1}{2} C(\Delta V)^2$, and $PE_{electric} = \frac{Q^2}{2C}$.

Practice

1a. 4.80×10^{-5} C
1b. 4.50×10^{-6} J
2a. 9.00 V
2b. 5.0×10^{-12} C

Review

1a. 8.8×10^{-13} F
1b. 5.3×10^{-12} C
2. If there is no potential difference, there is no electric force to set charges in motion.

SECTION 3 CURRENT AND RESISTANCE

1. Electrons can move freely through copper, so they easily respond to an electric field. Protons are bound to the nucleus of an atom, so they cannot be charge carriers in copper.
2. Since electrons are negatively charged, they move along a conductor in a direction opposite the electric field, **E.**
3. First determine the slope of the line by dividing the difference in y values between two points by the difference in x values between the two points. The slope is equal to $1/R$, so find the resistance by dividing 1 by the slope.

Practice

1. 4.00×10^2 s
2. 2.0×10^1 C
3. 0.43 A
4. 1.8 A
5. 1.10×10^2 V

Chapter 17 Electrical Energy and Current

Review

1. 12 A
2. 3.6 Ω
3. Although electrons experience a force that moves them across the conductor, collisions with atoms continually randomize their motion. As a result, the drift speed is much less than the average speed between collisions.
4. You could decrease current by making the wire as long as possible, thereby increasing its resistance.

SECTION 4 ELECTRIC POWER

1. When a potential difference is applied to a wire, the electrons move from a position of higher electric potential to a position of lower electric potential, and a current is produced in the circuit.
2. No; only alternating currents have a frequency. Direct currents do not change.
3. If the amount of time for a charge carrier to move through a circuit decreases while all other factors remain unchanged, then the power increases. Power is inversely proportional to the time.
4. Power companies transfer electrical energy at low currents and high potential differences to minimize I^2R losses.

Practice

1. 14 Ω
2. 1.5 V

Review

1. the rate at which electrical energy is delivered to the bulb, or the rate at which the bulb converts electrical energy to other forms of energy
2. It will decrease.
3. A low current minimizes the I^2R loss, making power transfer more efficient. Because $P = I\Delta V$, for a given amount of power, a low current corresponds to a high potential difference.

CHAPTER 17 REVIEW

1a. The positive charge moves in the direction of the electric field.
1b. The work done by the field on the charge converts electrical potential energy into kinetic energy.
2. 2.6×10^4 V
3. -4.2×10^5 V
4. $\pm 7.2 \times 10^{-11}$ C
5. 0.22 J
6. the current made of positive charge that has the same effect as the actual current
7. 2.0 s
8. c (greatest); a (least)
9. 0.20 A
10. 3.4 A
11. In dc, charges move in one direction, and in ac, charges oscillate; ac
12. 93 Ω
13. 0.62 A; 190 Ω

Chapter 18 Circuits and Elements

REVIEW PREVIOUS CONCEPTS

1. Potential difference is the work that must be done against electric forces to move a charge between the two points in question, divided by the charge.
2. Electric current is the rate at which electric charges move through an area.

SECTION 1 SCHEMATIC DIAGRAMS AND CIRCUITS

1. It is a diagram that shows how the components of an electrical device are connected.
2. It is a path that allows the flow of charges.

Review

1. one battery, one closed switch, two resistors, and three bulbs
2. The circuit should include the elements as they appear in the table of schematic diagram symbols.
3. 3.0 V
4. It is converted to thermal energy and light energy.

SECTION 2 RESISTORS IN SERIES OR IN PARALLEL

1. Equivalent resistance is the total resistance of multiple resistors combined in series or in parallel.
2. They are similar because there are loads, voltages, and current in both. They are different by how the loads are combined and the impact on the change in voltage and current when the loads are combined.

Practice

Aa. 43.6 Ω; 3.30 W
Ab. 0.275 A
B. 4.5 A, 2.2 A, 1.8 A, 1.3 A
C. 50.0 Ω

Review

1. in the series circuit
2a. All have equal I.
2b. 15 Ω
3. Because the resistance of each bulb is the same, the brightness depends only on the potential difference. Bulbs (a), (d), and (e) have an equal potential difference across

them and thus equal brightnesses. Because bulbs (b) and (c) have the same resistance and are in series, they have equal but lesser potential differences and are equally bright but less bright than bulbs (a), (d), and (e).

SECTION 3 COMPLEX RESISTOR COMBINATIONS

1. When current gets too high, the circuit breaker triggers a switch that opens the circuit.
2. A simplified circuit is a circuit diagram made by reducing a more complex circuit into series and parallel branches, and finding equivalent resistances.

Practice

Aa. 27.8 Ω
Ab. 26.6 Ω
Ba. Ra: 0.50 A, 2.5 V
Bb. R_b: 0.50 A, 3.5 V
Bc. R_c: 1.5 A, 6.0 V
Bd. R_d: 1.0 A, 4.0 V
Be. R_e: 1.0 A, 4.0 V
Bf. R_f: 2.0 A, 4.0 V

Review

1. 175 Ω
2. 0.229 A, 3.44 V
3. 0.235 A, 3.52 V

CHAPTER 18 REVIEW

1. Schematic diagrams are useful because they summarize the contents of an electric circuit.
2. 12.0 V
3. The circuit is not complete or the resistance is too great.
4. all; D
5. b
6. a
7a. 24 Ω
7b. 1.0 A
8a. 2.99 Ω
8b. 4.0 A
9a. 13.3 Ω
9b. 0.902 A
9c. 1.4 V
10. 28 V

Chapter 19 Magnetism

REVIEW PREVIOUS CONCEPTS
1. a net force
2. rotation
3. multiply the force and the lever arm
4. the rate at which electric charges move through a cross-sectional area

SECTION 1 MAGNETS AND MAGNETIC FIELDS
1. They repel one another.
2. In ferromagnetic materials, the magnetic fields produced by electron spins do not cancel completely.
3. No; Some unmagnetized materials have magnetic domains that are oriented randomly.
4. to the right
5. a magnetic north pole

Review
1a. attract
1b. repel
1c. attract
2. two
3. a, b
4. parallel to Earth's surface, pointing from approximately the geographic South Pole (magnetic north pole) to approximately the geographic North Pole (magnetic south pole)
5. hard magnetic materials, because they are less easily magnetized

SECTION 2 MAGNETISM FROM ELECTRICITY
1. counterclockwise
2. The strength of the magnetic field decreases.
3. The direction of the magnetic field is reversed.
4. no, because the period is proportional to the square root of the mass

Review
1. concentric circles around the wire
2. The fields produced by the top and bottom of every loop all point in the same direction and are confined to a small region of space.
3. Electrons usually pair up with their spins opposite each other, and their magnetic fields cancel each other.
4. Yes, the north pole of the solenoid would point to Earth's geographic North Pole. No, the solenoid would oscillate back and forth as its poles continually reversed.

SECTION 3 MAGNETIC FORCE
1. If the charge is not moving and if the charge moves along the field lines.
2. the tesla (T)
3. The fingers indicate the direction of the magnetic field. The palm indicates the direction of the magnetic force.
4. when the currents are in the same direction

Practice
A. 3.57×10^6 m/s
B. 0.70 A
C. 0.59 m

Review
1. 0.081 T
2. upward
3. 0.75 N
4. attractive

CHAPTER 19 REVIEW
1. The geographic North Pole is near Earth's magnetic south pole.
2. The added energy causes the domains to become less aligned.
3. south
4. number of coils per unit length, amount of current
5. The proton would go left, and the electron would go right.
6. The magnetic field from one wire is perpendicular to the second wire (and thus the current in it) at the second wire's location. The magnetic force on the second wire is away from the first wire.
7. 15 m/s
8a. to the left
8b. into the page
8c. out of the page
8d. up the page
9a. to the left
9b. into the page
9c. out of the page
9d. up the page
10. 8.0×10^{-3} T, in the positive z direction
11. 8.0 m/s

Chapter 20 Electromagnetic Induction

REVIEW PREVIOUS CONCEPTS

1. The current is proportional to the applied potential difference.
2. The current is inversely proportional to the resistance of the circuit.

SECTION 1 ELECTRICITY FROM MAGNETISM

1. an electric current
2. The emf moves the charges in the wire like the potential difference supplied by a battery.
3. The loop should be turned to be parallel to the magnetic field.
4. attractive
5. The current stops flowing.
6. The minus sign indicates that the magnetic field of the induced current is in the opposite direction of any change that affects that field.

Practice

1. emf = 0.11 V
2. 14 A

Review

1. Answers will vary. Sample answer: Electromagnetic induction is changing the magnetic field through a circuit to cause an electric current to flow.
2. Answers should include any three of the following: moving the loop into or out of the magnetic field; rotating the loop within the magnetic field; changing the strength of the magnetic field through the static loop; altering the loop's shape.
3. 0.21 V
4. When the magnetized strings vibrate, the strength of their magnetic field changes periodically with respect to the wire loops in the coil, inducing an emf in the coil. The fluctuations in the induced current match the frequencies and amplitudes of the sounds produced on the vibrating strings.

SECTION 2 GENERATORS, MOTORS, AND MUTUAL INDUCTANCE

1. Mechanical energy that turns a loop is converted to electrical energy.
2. Points b and d are farthest up or down the vertical emf value axis from the zero point, which is where the time axis crosses. They are the points where the plot reverses direction.
3. An ac generator has two slip rings, but the dc generator has one slip ring, called a commutator.
4. The plot for a dc generator does not look like a sine wave because there are no negative values plotted.
5. The current regularly reverses and is always repelled by the fixed magnetic field.
6. The back emf opposes the induced current in a coil and tends to reduce the current.
7. Mutual inductance is when one circuit induces an emf in a nearby circuit when the current through the circuit is changing.

Review

1. A generator is a device that converts mechanical energy into electrical energy.
2. 120 V
3. Maximum mutual inductance takes place when the planes of the two loops are parallel. Minimum mutual inductance takes place when the planes of the loops are perpendicular to each other.

SECTION 3 AC CIRCUITS AND TRANSFORMERS

1. Δv is the induced emf and Δv_{max} is the maximum emf in an ac circuit.
2. ac current stays at I_{max} for only an instant.
3. You need one current value and the resistance of the circuit.
4. Answers may vary. You would use a step-down transformer to reduce the emf. For example, step-down transformers are used to bring the high voltage from a power line down to 110 V for household use.
5. The automobile may not start or run.

Practice

A. 4.8 A; 6.8 A, 170 V
B. 7.8 A
C. 1.44 A; 2.04 A, 21.2 V
Da. 1.10×10^2 V
Db. 2.1 A
E. 6.9×10^4 V
F. 3.5×10^4 turns
G. 147 V

Review

1. An rms current is the amount of alternating current that heats as much as the same amount of dc current heats.
2. 0.035 mA; 0.11 V; 0.15 V
3. 1.7×10^4 V
4. Zero; the current is positive for exactly the same amount of time that it is negative. The direction of current (positive or negative) does not affect the heating of the resistor. That is, the resistor is being heated throughout the cycle whether the current is positive or negative.

SECTION 4 ELECTROMAGNETIC WAVES

1. Electromagnetic waves are produced by oscillating electric and magnetic fields.
2. electric force and magnetic force
3. Low-energy photons act more like waves, and high-energy photons act more like particles.
4. The energy of electromagnetic radiation is directly proportional to frequency.
5. The human eye can see only a very small part of the spectrum, between 700 nm and 400 nm.
6. Gamma rays have very high energy, enough to kill cancerous cells.

Review

1. Answers may vary. Electromagnetic radiation is the energy transferred by all types of electromagnetic waves.
2. Maxwell's equations predicted that a changing magnetic field would produce an electric field. Maxwell's equations also predicted that light was electromagnetic radiation.
3. Both act on charged particles. Both are considered aspects of a single electromagnetic force.
4. frequency, wavelength, and energy
5. The energy of electromagnetic waves is stored in the electric and magnetic fields that make up the wave. The energy can be added to materials to increase their energy, such as the heating of food.

CHAPTER 20 REVIEW

1. Place plane of coil perpendicular to magnetic field and move it into or out of field, rotate coil about axis perpendicular to magnetic field, and change strength of magnetic field with variable resistor.
2. Answers could be three of the following: magnetic field component perpendicular to plane of coil; area of coil; time in which changes occur; number of turns of wire in coil.
3. By opposing changes in the external field, the induced B field prevents the system's energy from increasing or decreasing.
4. no; Effects of one magnet cancel those of the other magnet.
5. 0.12 A
6. B field (induces emf in turning coil), wire coil (conducts induced current), slip rings (maintain contact with rest of circuit by means of conducting brushes)
7. turn the handle faster
8. an emf with polarity opposite that of the emf powering the motor; The coil's rotation in the B field induces a back emf that reduces the net potential difference across the motor.
9. The changing B field produced by a changing current in one circuit induces an emf and current in a nearby circuit.
10. The magnetic forces are greatest on charges in the sides of a loop that move perpendicular to the B field (that is, when the plane of the loop is parallel to the field lines).
11a. 8.34 A
11b. 119 V
12. frequency, maximum current, and maximum voltage
13. The rms values are preferred because they give the same heating effect as the same value of direct current.
14. 48 turns
15. Changing electric and magnetic fields are at right angles to each other and to the direction in which the electromagnetic wave moves.
16. An electron takes longer to travel the length of a long antenna than a short one. Since the velocity of both lengths of waves will be the speed of light, the wave's frequency will be smaller.

Chapter 21 Atomic Physics

REVIEW PREVIOUS CONCEPTS

1. Standing waves are wave patterns that result when two waves of the same frequency, wavelength, and amplitude travel in opposite directions and interfere. Standing waves have stationary nodes and antinodes.

2. Electromagnetic waves consist of coupled changing electric and magnetic fields. They move through space at the speed of light.

3. Visible light is the wavelengths of electromagnetic radiation that are visible to the human eye. The comprise the section of the electromagnetic spectrum with wavelengths between infrared and ultraviolet.

SECTION 1 QUANTIZATION OF ENERGY

1. infrared

2. Sample response: electric charge from light

3. the frequency above which the photoelectric effect is observed

4. Discrete states proceed in steps—a quantity can be one or the other, but not in between. In a continuous state, there is always another state in between two states.

Practice

A. 1.2×10^{15} Hz

B. 1.32×10^{-3} eV

C. 2.3 eV; 5.6×10^{14} Hz

D. yes

Review

1. whether the effect occurred; how fast it occurred; the maximum kinetic energy of the electrons; the number of electrons; Only the last depends on intensity; the others depend on the frequency of the light.

2. 2.8 eV

3. blue light; Red light has a longer wavelength and so shorter frequency, and so by $E = hf$ less energy.

SECTION 2 MODELS OF THE ATOM

1. toward the center of a circular path; It causes it to change direction.

2. the atomic gas enclosed in the tube

3. those whose energy matches the separation between energy levels

Practice

A. 4.56×10^{14} Hz; the fourth line

B. 1.61×10^{15} Hz

C. 3.02 eV; E_6 to E_2; the first line

Review

1. Because most alpha particles were not deflected at all, while a few were sharply deflected.

2. Isolate the light from a star, and find the absorption spectrum. Compare this to the spectra for known elements.

3. The light is limited to the wavelengths produced when the electrons in atoms in the atmosphere, such as nitrogen or oxygen, jump between allowed levels. Because the energy change between allowed levels is not continuous, the wavelengths produced are not continuous.

SECTION 3 QUANTUM MECHANICS

1. 1.7×10^{-17} J

2. Answers will vary but should equal $8/n$ m, where n is a natural number. Sample response: 4 m, 2 m, 1 m

3. The most probable locations in Schrödinger's model are the Bohr radii.

Practice

A. 1.46×10^3 m/s

B. 8.84×10^{-27} m/s

Review

1. The allowed orbits are those that contain an integral number of electron wavelenths.

2. 3.96×10^{-11} m/

3. The electron cloud of possible locations reflects that the electron's location cannot be known with precision.

4. According to Heisenberg's uncertainty principle, below a certain limit increased precision in measuring location will be offset by increased uncertainty in measuring momentum, and vice versa. It is a limit in nature, not in the tools used to study nature.

CHAPTER 21 REVIEW

1. Because the discrepancy happens at the ultraviolet end of the spectrum, where instead of moving toward infinity radiation drops to zero.

2. No, the threshold frequency above which the photoelectric effect takes place is unique for each metal.

3. The electron can only be at certain orbital levels, not between them.

4. 4.72 eV

5. 9.8×10^{-35} m

6. the possible locations of an electron around a nucleus

7. Each line corresponds to a transition between energy levels. All of the transitions in the absorption spectrum (ground state to excited) are found in the emission spectrum (excited state to ground).

8. 3.16×10^{15} Hz

9. 2.49×10^{-5} eV

10. Spectral lines correspond to jumps between stable orbits.

11. Yes; if the photon and electron exchange energy and momentum in the collision, then the energy of the photon changes. This means that the frequency, and so the wavelength, of the photon also changes.

12. Planck assumed that energy is quantized; classical physics assumed that energy is continuous.

Chapter 22 Subatomic Physics

REVIEW PREVIOUS CONCEPTS

1. The modern model of the atom has a dense nucleus in the center and an electron cloud in orbitals around the nucleus.

2. Light can show interference patterns (waves) and act as quanta of energy (particles).

SECTION 1 THE NUCLEUS

1. Atomic mass is the combined number of protons and neutrons. The atomic number is just the number of protons.

2. The equation shows how mass and energy can be converted to each other.

3. As the number of protons increases, the number of neutrons needs to increase to stabilize the nucleus. At some point, the neutrons cannot balance the repulsion of the protons and no isotopes are stable.

Practice

A. Carbon 12 is more stable because the ratio of protons to neutrons is closer to 1:1.

B. The most stable isotope of calcium is Ca-40. Calcium has a mass of 40 and an atomic number of 20 so it has 20 neutrons; a 1:1 ratio.

Review

1. the charge of the nucleus (the atomic number)

2. They have the same number of protons and electrons. They have different numbers of neutrons and hence different numbers of nucleons.

3. Z is the same for each isotope; A and N are different.

4. the strong force

5. For light nuclei, $N \approx Z$. As the number of protons (Z) increases, more neutrons per proton are needed to compensate for the Coulomb repulsion—so $N > Z$.

6. six; eight; six

SECTION 2 NUCLEAR DECAY

1. They are different because each type of decay releases a different particle, sometimes changing into another isotope. They are similar because each decay results in an increase in the stability of the nucleus.

2. The parent nuclei is the isotope before a decay event. The daughter nuclei is the nucleus that is left over after a decay event, more stable than the parent nuclei.

3. The half-life is the time it takes for one-half of a radioactive sample to decay.

Practice

A. $^{208}_{81}\text{Tl}$ (Thallium)

B. 1.0 h

C. **a.** about 5.0×10^7 atoms
   b. about 3.5×10^8 atoms

Review

1. In α, ^{24}He particles are emitted; in β, electrons or positrons are emitted; in γ, photons are emitted. In α and β, a new element is produced; in γ, energy is lost.

2. **a.** $^{228}_{88}\text{Ra}$
   b. $^{12}_{6}\text{C}$
   c. $^{149}_{62}\text{Sm}$

3. 17, 140 years

SECTION 3 NUCLEAR REACTIONS

1. Fission is the splitting of nuclei into lighter nuclei.

2. A controlled reaction proceeds slowly. An uncontrolled reaction results in the release of an enormous amount of energy and an explosion.

3. Fusion is the combining of nuclei to form a heavier nucleus.

Review

1. Both are nuclear reactions that release energy. In fission, a heavy nucleus splits; in fusion, two light nuclei combine.

2. Enrichment is the process of increasing the amount of ^{235}U in reactor fuels. This is necessary because uranium from ore contains mostly ^{238}U.

3. **a.** $^{1}_{0}n + {}^{235}_{92}\text{U} \longrightarrow {}^{141}_{56}\text{Ba} + {}^{92}_{36}\text{Kr} + 3\,^{1}_{0}n$
   b. three neutrons

4. Fusion reactors produce less radioactive waste, and the fuel (water) is plentiful. Difficulties include the high temperatures and densities necessary to achieve controlled fusion reactions.

5. A fusion reactor produces less radioactive waste than a fission reactor because fusion produces nuclei that are more stable than the nuclei produced by fission.

SECTION 4 PARTICLE PHYSICS

1. Strong force holds nucleons together. Weak force causes beta decay. Electromagnetic force affects charged particles. Gravitational force affects all masses over very long distances.

2. Leptons are electrons and neutrinos; baryons are protons and neutrons. Leptons are thought to be fundamental particles, while baryons are made up of quarks.

Review

1. The strong force is carried by gluons, the electromagnetic force is carried by photons, the weak force is carried by W and Z bosons, and gravity is carried by gravitons.

2. Hadrons consist of quarks, while leptons are thought to be indivisible. Hadrons interact with gluons (the strong interaction), but leptons do not. Mesons consist of one quark and one antiquark, and baryons consist of three quarks.

3. Up to 10^{-43} s, all forces were unified. At 10^{-43} s, gravity broke free; at 10^{-32} s, the strong force broke free; and at 10^{-10} s, the weak force broke free. From 10^{-43} s to 10^{-32} s, quarks, leptons, and their antiparticles existed. Until 70 000 years (2×10^{12} s), most energy was in the form of radiation. At 380 000 years (1×10^{13} s), atoms began forming. Soon most energy was in the form of matter, as it is today.

CHAPTER 22 REVIEW

1. 79; 118; 79

2. Isotopes are atoms with the same Z but different N and A.

3. the strong force

4. because of a greater Coulomb repulsion between the protons

5. Alpha decay emits a helium nucleus, causes a new element to form, and decreases the mass of the parent nucleus. Beta decay emits an electron, causes a new element to form but does not decrease the mass. Gamma decay emits a high-energy photon and results in energy released but no change in mass or atomic number.

6. For each α, A decreases by four, and Z decreases by two. For each $\beta-$, A stays the same, and Z increases by one.

7. the high temperatures and densities required

8. The amount of C-14 left undecayed is too small to be measured accurately.

9. $^{10}_{5}\text{B}$

10. $^{4}_{2}\text{He}$

11. 22,860 years old

12. Quarks make up hadrons; they have fractional charge, have never been isolated, and are attracted to one another by the strong force.

13. The photon is a mediating field particle for the electromagnetic force, while the neutrino is a particle emitted in beta decay.

14. Yes; hadrons consist of mesons and baryons. Thus, all mesons are hadrons, but not all hadrons are mesons; some are baryons.

15. 2 neutrons

16. $^{8}_{4}\text{Be}$